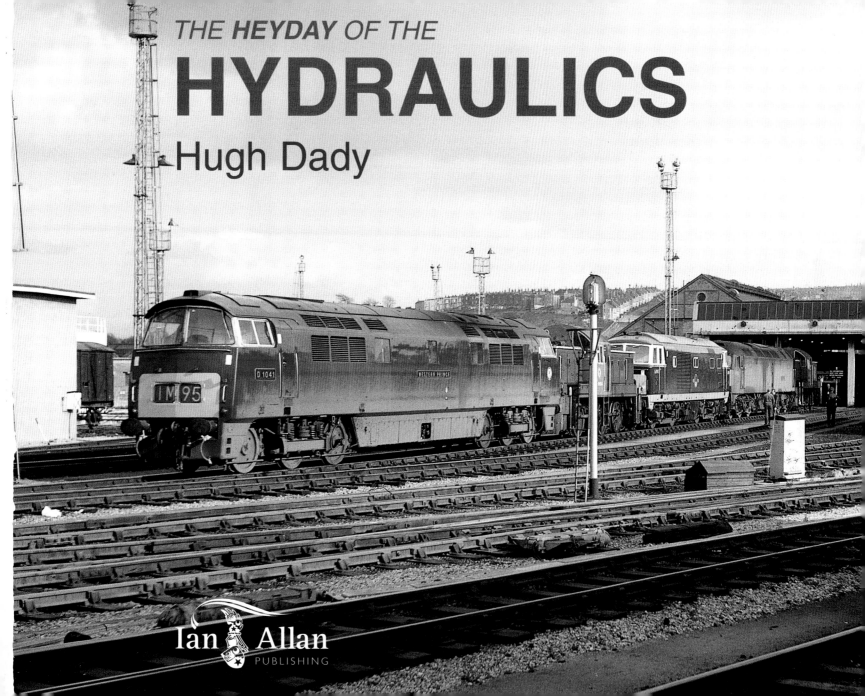

THE *HEYDAY* OF THE
HYDRAULICS
Hugh Dady

Ian Allan PUBLISHING

First published 2010

ISBN 978 0 7110 3440 2

© Ian Allan Publishing 2010

Published by Ian Allan Publishing

an imprint of Ian Allan Publishing Ltd, Hersham, Surrey, KT12 4RG
Printed in England by Ian Allan Printing Ltd, Hersham, Surrey, KT12 4RG

Distributed in Canada and the United States of America by BookMasters Distribution Services

Code: 1005/B1

Visit the Ian Allan Publishing website at www.ianallanpublishing.com

Front cover: No D7063 heads a Bristol–Weymouth excursion train south of Yeovil Pen Mill on 2 June 1963. In the background is the Yeovil Town–Yeovil Junction branch. *John Beckett*

Back cover: No D1067 *Western Druid* climbs away from Bath with the 11.15 Bristol–Paddington on 10 June 1968. *The Revd Alan Newman*

Previous page: Bristol Bath Road plays host to a variety of hydraulics on 20 April 1966. Leading the line-up is No D1041 *Western Prince* standing in front of No D9554 and a recently ex-works 'Hymek'. *The Revd Alan Newman*

Below: Still fitted with miniature snowploughs from the winter, No D7000 waits to leave Mangotsfield with the 12.10 (SO) Bristol Temple Meads–Bath Green Park on the last day of the service, 5 March 1966. *Russell Leitch*

Right: Having just cleared the summit of Dainton Bank, a pair of 'Warships', No D832 *Onslaught* leading, begin the downhill stretch to Newton Abbot with the up 'Cornish Riviera' on 29 November 1969. *Peter Gray*

Introduction

When the Modernisation Plan for British Railways was announced in January 1955 the Western Region looked forward to an opportunity to transform and accelerate its services. The few contemporary diesels in the UK were of similar or lower power output than the steam locomotives they were intended to replace, so the WR looked to developments unfolding in Europe, and in particular Germany. Here it found that considerable success was being achieved with high-speed lightweight diesels fitted with hydraulic transmission.

Alone among the Regions that made up British Railways, the Western sought and obtained permission to pursue hydraulic transmission for its main-line diesel fleet, ordered by the British Transport Commission under the auspices of the Modernisation Plan.

For the enthusiast, the decision provided a unique spectacle that appeared to keep the individual spirit of the old GWR alive. High-revving engines gave a distinctive sound, while the naming of the Type 4s continued a long tradition. Careful styling produced shapes for the 'Hymeks' and 'Westerns' that still look 'modern' 50 years after they were conceived.

In truth, the hydraulic flirtation was probably doomed from the start by numbers alone. The idea of one Region running an entirely different diesel fleet on part of a supposedly unified system seemed at odds with the policy pursued only a few years previously, when BR had introduced a range of 'standard' steam designs for use across the country. Perhaps the real mistake was that, instead of detailed testing and evaluation of hydraulic transmission with a small batch of 'Pilot Scheme' locomotives, as had been intended, acceleration of the Modernisation Plan saw some 365 locomotives ordered straight from the drawing board.

By the mid-1960s, as traffic declined, it was clear that British Railways had over-estimated the number of diesels it required. A National Traction Policy emerged which envisaged the elimination of non-standard classes. The hydraulics were an obvious target, with inevitable implications for the workshops that undertook main overhauls. Even so, enthusiasts at the time showed little interest as the first North British-built classes slipped away for scrap. The Swindon-built 'Warships' followed without any farewell, but at least the 'Hymeks' were accorded a (rather premature) swansong special. Then came the turn of the 'Westerns', and suddenly it was as though the nation's railway enthusiasts had woken from hibernation! Happily today's generation can enjoy the sight and sound of all but the North British classes in preservation.

This collection provides a glimpse of the 19-year spell of diesel-hydraulics at work on BR. As ever, my grateful thanks to the photographers concerned for allowing me to search their collections and portray in colour the early diesel era, which now seems as remote as the steam age it succeeded.

Hugh Dady
Dawlish
March 2010

The ultimate development of the diesel-hydraulic for the Western Region, the 'Western' C-C, would prove to be much the most popular type among enthusiasts, particularly in later years. When new, the classic shape developed with consultants from the Design Research Unit (DRU) was the subject of several livery experiments. No D1000 *Western Enterprise* emerged from Swindon Works in December 1961 in a shade referred to as 'Desert Sand'. The colour was said to associate with the sand of beaches in the West Country, but this seems a rather tenuous link. The advantage was that such a pale colour was visible to trackside workers, but it proved very difficult to keep clean. On 1 September 1962 the locomotive passes the junction at Savernake for Marlborough with train 1A67, the 9.20am Falmouth–Paddington. *Mike Pope*

Many enthusiasts probably best remember the class at work in the final corporate blue livery of British Rail. Although blue did not suit many classes, the 'Westerns' seemed to look good in almost any colour scheme. Ironically the DRU had favoured blue from new, albeit a different shade, and was dead against the maroon livery initially chosen by public competition. In this scene, recorded from the road bridge adjacent to Westbury station, No D1020 *Western Hero* comes off the line from Bradford Junction with train 6V53, the Etruria–St Blazey china-clay empties, on 16 May 1969. At this time the train was regularly routed via Oxford, Chippenham and Melksham, but in later years it would return via Cheltenham and Bristol.

The Revd Alan Newman

The largest hydraulic class and arguably the most successful was the 101-strong fleet of B-B locomotives built by Beyer Peacock & Co at its Gorton works in Manchester. They were handsome-looking machines, thanks to styling and livery advice from Wilkes & Ashmore of Horsham, and quickly earned a good reputation in service. The initial order, for 45 locomotives, was followed by another, for 50, before the first had been completed. New locomotives were trialled over the Peak line to Derby, and

in this view at the station on 27 June 1962 No D7041 awaits return with its trial load to Manchester, where any final adjustments would be made before despatch to Swindon. The term 'Hymek', which was formally added to the name Beyer Peacock, was short for the hydro-mechanical Mekydro transmission and quickly became the accepted description used for these locomotives.

Alec Swain / M. Wroblewski collection

'Hymeks' were delivered to Swindon for acceptance and were usually given further shakedown trials either to Stoke Gifford or over the route to Gloucester via Kemble. The latter included the very attractive stretch between Sapperton and Stroud known as the Golden Valley, which became a regular stamping-ground for the class.

On 19 October 1963 the surroundings were certainly living up to their name as a 'Hymek' approached Brimscombe Bridge halt with a local from Swindon to Gloucester. *John Beckett*

Swindon is often remembered as the birthplace and home of diesel-hydraulics working on British Railways. However, it is interesting to note that only a third of the WR's 365-strong hydraulic fleet was actually constructed at the Works. Private industry won contracts to build more than half the fleet as well as the supply of all engines, transmissions, boilers and cooler groups for locomotives constructed in the railway workshops. In this view of 'A' shop at Swindon, recorded on 3 May 1959, the 'Warship' production line has briefly fallen silent, this being a Sunday.

The bodyshell of No D811 (to be) stands surrounded by scaffold towers. Behind are Nos D810/09/8/7 and No D806 in green undercoat. Steam locomotives were still being built and overhauled and appear to have been slotted in between the diesel production line. The 'Warships' were the first locomotives in the UK to employ stressed-skin construction, whereby all of the body panels and structure were load-bearing. This eliminated the need for a separate underframe of large section and enabled considerable weight saving. *Trevor Owen*

The finished product in the shape of No D802 *Formidable*, last of the Pilot Scheme locomotives, enters Saltash with an up service in August 1959. The production run of 'Warships', starting with No D803, was actually sanctioned and the build started long before the first of the Pilot Scheme locomotives had taken to the rails. As a result, modifications shown to be necessary because of early service experience had to be applied on the hoof — an expensive and frustrating activity that was impossible to hide from public attention. *R. C. Riley*

Above: Black sheep among the hydraulic classes were generally considered to be those locomotives built by the North British Locomotive Co (NBL). Circumstances seemed to conspire against this once-respected steam locomotive builder. Its first products, in the shape of five 2,000hp heavyweight A-1-A 'Warships', were largely unwanted as a result of policy disagreements between the British Transport Commission and the WR, which preferred to opt for a lightweight German design. It was unfortunate that NBL had taken out licensing agreements with MAN for the engines, as the Deutsche Bundesbahn subsequently confirmed that of the three engine types used in its 'V200s', the MAN found least favour. On 15 May 1959 No D603 *Conquest* looks to have been the subject of recent cleaning as it passes the steam shed and enters Truro with the up 'Cornish Riviera Express'. *Michael Mensing*

Above right: First of the production run of North British Type 2s, No D6306 approaches Cowley Bridge Junction on 4 July 1961 with Southern Bulleid coaches forming an exchange working from Exeter to Plymouth via Okehampton. It had been policy for some years for Southern and Western crews to work over each other's routes between Exeter and Plymouth to remain familiar should one be blocked by severe weather. *R. C. Riley*

Right: On 30 August 1961 North British-built No D853 *Thruster* had just arrived at what was to be its first home, the new and yet to be fully opened diesel depot at Laira, Plymouth. The locomotive has been attached to dynamometer car No DW150192, a Hawksworth passenger coach that had been converted for diesel-locomotive testing by the Western Region in May 1961. Until the new facility was formally opened later in the year most diesel servicing continued at the old steam shed, visible on the extreme right. *R. C. Riley*

11

The route from Hereford and Worcester to Paddington enjoyed a long association with the 'Hymeks', although they were largely displaced by North British 'Warships' between 1968 and 1971. On 2 June 1963 No D7076, just a month old, still looks smart as it sets off from Worcester for Hereford with a train from Paddington. Withdrawn after exactly 10 years in front-line service, No D7076 would be retained (along with No D7096) for dead-load testing by the Railway Technical Centre at Derby. Although it was little used at the Old Dalby test location, its migration north allowed the locomotive to escape the cutting-up process at Swindon. After a further 10 years, in 1983, No D7076 was purchased by the Bury Hydraulic Group and moved to the East Lancashire Railway, where extensive restoration was undertaken, and has since visited a number of preserved railways in addition to seeing regular use in Lancashire. *R. C. Riley*

Pictured on a warm early-autumn day, Brimscombe station looks to have seen better days. In the distance the once-busy goods yard is closed and the track partially recovered as No D7012 approaches with a Cheltenham–Swindon local on 6 October 1964. At this time the 'Hymeks' worked both the locals and the few Cheltenham St James–Paddington trains, but much of the service would soon be downgraded to DMUs working only as far as Swindon. *R. C. Riley*

13

Above: The 'Warships' spearheaded the Western Region's aim to eliminate steam from Devon and Cornwall at the earliest opportunity. The design was very much a copy of the German 'V200', scaled down to fit the British loading-gauge. Swindon would ultimately build just over half the fleet, construction of the remainder being entrusted to the North British Locomotive Co at Glasgow. On 2 May 1961 No D827 *Kelly* climbs the gradient into Bodmin Road with train 1M99, the 12.00 Penzance–Crewe. This was a mixed train conveying a small number of passenger coaches in Cornwall followed by a lengthy rake of vans. In the sidings can be seen wooden-bodied china-clay wagons for use on the Wenford branch. *R. C. Riley*

Right: Heading up the Berks & Hants at Wolf Hall Junction, a Swindon 'Warship' has charge of train 1A47, the 9.45am Churston–Paddington, on 1 September 1962. The lines to the left form the connection from the GW (Savernake) to the M&SWJR in the Andover direction. The photograph has been taken from the abutment of the M&SWJR line crossing the Great Western to Savernake High Level. *Mike Pope*

Left: No D1015 *Western Champion* speeds south on the through lines at Gerrards Cross on 27 April 1963 with train 1V03, the 7.40am Birkenhead–Paddington, overtaking what appears to be a school special in the platform road. The unique golden-ochre livery applied to No D1015 makes for an interesting comparison with the maroon BR coaching stock of the special. The maroon eventually adopted as standard for the 'Westerns' was exactly the same shade, being a mix of red oxide of iron with crimson lake, although the application differed; on locomotives this normally consisted of a priming coat, an undercoat, an enamel coat — in an attempt to provide resistance against heat and oil — and a coat of varnish, whereas coaches, after priming and undercoating, were given a coat of finishing colour and then up to three coats of varnish to protect the various transfers.
Alec Swain / M. Wroblewski collection

Above: No D1027 *Western Lancer* arrives at Truro with the down 'Royal Duchy' on 16 September 1964. It was still the practice at this date to change locomotives at Plymouth on services to/from Paddington, the much-reduced load over the Cornish section meaning that 'Warships' were the staple motive power for most services in the far West. *Western Lancer* had entered traffic from Laira in January 1964 and would be withdrawn in November 1975, having completed 1,176,000 miles in just under 12 years. *David Pool*

Above left: No D6308 stands at Laira steam shed in original condition on 25 September 1960. Some of the diesels were still subjected to cleaning by hand, which probably accounts for the respectable condition of the locomotive after nine months in traffic. Note, above the front cab windows, the additional air vents which were a feature of Nos D6300-12 and D6333. *R. C. Riley*

Left: Just three weeks old, No D6339 approaches Wadebridge on 24 April 1962 with a train from Bodmin General. Delivery of the production series, which had begun in October 1959, became very protracted as North British was asked to concentrate on the 'D833' series of 'Warships'. By the end of 1960 the class had reached No D6334, yet during 1961 only two further examples were added. After a lull of eight months

No D6337 appeared in March 1962, and the class was completed with No D6357 in November of that year, the build of 52 locomotives having spanned more than three years. *John Beckett*

Above: Photographers recording the last day of passenger services on the Dulverton–Stoke Cannon Exe Valley line were disappointed to find a North British Type 2 and six coaches replacing the usual '14xx' and autotrain. Under gathering clouds, No D6348 leaves Bampton on 5 October 1963 with the afternoon train for Tiverton and Exeter. This was one of the final batch of 'D63xx' locomotives, delivered with yellow warning panels, and vertical grab-rails above the split headcode boxes. *Michael Messenger*

Above: On 30 April 1963 various publicity photographs were taken at Landore ahead of the official opening three days later of the newly constructed diesel depot. The two principal hydraulic classes operating in Wales, represented by No D1045 *Western Viscount* and No D7022, make an interesting comparison with newly delivered Type 3 diesel-electric No D6833. *Philip Kelley collection*

Below: Initial teething troubles with the 'Westerns' saw 'Hymeks' standing in on many of the London–South Wales expresses. By 1964 diagrams had been recast, and Brush Type 4s had replaced 'Westerns' on the WR Paddington–Birmingham route. This in turn allowed the hydraulic Type 4s to take over from the 'Hymeks' on several Cardiff and Swansea diagrams, which they would share with increasing numbers of Brush Type 4s. On 13 July 1964 green-liveried No D1035 *Western Yeoman* arrives at Cardiff with the 12.20pm Swansea–Paddington. *Geoff Lendon*

After initial deliveries to Bristol Bath Road, South Wales gained a significant allocation of 'Hymeks' from early 1962. One of the lesser-known routes from which they displaced steam was that between Carmarthen and Aberystwyth. On a dank and dismal 27 December 1963 the steam leaking from the coaches of the mid-day train to Carmarthen looks very welcoming as No D7080 waits to head south from Aberystwyth over the 56-mile route. The number of halts in the more remote parts of West Wales meant that well over two hours was allowed for this journey. *Trevor Owen*

Below: Another member of the class has an easy job on 15 June 1964 as it powers away from Aberystwyth with just two coaches forming the 11.55 to Carmarthen. Seeing only three services a day in each direction, the route was inevitably earmarked for closure, but flooding at the end of 1964 severed the line and provided a convenient excuse for early closure of a major section of the route. *John Beckett*

Above: Freight services of the mid-1960s followed a pattern quite different from those of today, a number of general-merchandise trains calling at major yards *en route* before reaching their destination. One such working was train 6V02, the 08.00 Poole–Severn Tunnel Junction, seen here on 28 May 1966 near Avoncliff behind No D860 *Victorious*. The service took much of the day to reach South Wales, and before the advent of computerised records using TOPS it was quite common for individual wagons to be mislaid in the yards, sometimes for days at a time. The Beeching cuts and the growth of road transport ensured that the pick-up feeder freights connecting with these trunk services were in rapid decline, so it was only a matter of time before trains such as 6V02 were discontinued. *The Revd Alan Newman*

Right: The hydraulics were no strangers to working 'off-region', and a number of services were so diagrammed despite the very different traction knowledge required. When the ex-LSWR route between Exeter and Salisbury came under WR control it was decided that the Western would become responsible for traction over the entire route to London, and from August 1964 'Warships' began a seven-year reign working between Exeter and Waterloo. Swindon-built locomotives were used because of their better reliability — particularly important over the route's long single-line sections — while the stock was a mix of Bulleid and BR Mk1 coaches. In this view at Deepcut, between Farnborough and Brookwood, No D824 *Highflyer* heads a mix of liveries and coach types forming the 10.20 Exeter–Waterloo in June 1967. *Mike Pope*

22

Above: No D9511 demonstrates the haulage capability of the type at Pontypool Road on 14 April 1967. The Class 14s, as they were eventually designated, simply arrived too late for British Railways; there had been a number of false starts over the design of a small Type 1 hydraulic, and by the time the engineering configuration had been settled, the traffic for which they had been intended had hæmorrhaged so badly that they should never really have been built. The main beneficiaries were the coal and steel industries, in which the majority of locomotives found employment after their premature withdrawal. Discarded by BR in April 1968, No D9511 would be sold to the National Coal Board (NCB) at Ashington, where it was to give a further 10 years' service before being cut up in the summer of 1979. *The Revd Alan Newman*

Right: No D9500 stands in the sidings adjacent to the Lister Diesels factory at Dursley with a trip working from Gloucester on 16 May 1966. New to traffic on 24 July 1964, No D9500 would be among the final batch listed for withdrawal on 26 April 1969. In practice the official withdrawal dates need to be viewed with caution, because some locomotives were briefly reactivated for trial on BR metals before being sold on to new industrial owners. No D9500 was another candidate for the NCB at Ashington but has fortunately lived on into the world of preservation. *Bill Potter / R. W. Carroll collection*

Two 'Westerns', Nos D1010 and D1041, were involved in hauling the Royal Train around Wiltshire and Somerset during a two-day tour of Crown estates in 1966. After berthing overnight on the stub of the branch to Devizes, No D1041

Western Prince passes Hawkeridge Junction on the morning of 3 June 1966, transporting HM The Queen and HRH The Duke of Edinburgh to Castle Cary for a visit to the Royal Bath & West Show. *The Revd Alan Newman*

Resting between duties on 1 June 1966, No D821 *Greyhound* shows off its recently applied coat of maroon at Bristol Bath Road. Although this colour had been chosen for the 'Westerns' as early as 1962, it would be September 1965 before the first 'Warships' were so repainted. This livery change is difficult to explain, because in 1964 British Railways had already unveiled a new corporate blue livery on its 'XP64' train; moreover, no attempt seems to have been made to apply maroon to either the 'Hymeks' or the 'D6xx' 'Warships', which retained their locomotive green until the advent of Monastral blue, which colour (better known as Rail blue) was used from the autumn of 1966 for repaints of all classes. *The Revd Alan Newman*

Above: No D7084 ambles towards Trowbridge with the 14.00 Weymouth–Bristol parcels on 29 July 1966. There was still a large network of parcels traffic before today's road-based courier companies captured the market. Railway parcels (as distinct from those carried for the General Post Office) were a high-value part of what was termed 'sundries' traffic. Parcels could be booked in and collected from an office at many stations where a set of platform scales was usually seen outside the office. The parcels were conveyed in the luggage vans of scheduled passenger services and/or dedicated trains of GUVs, Siphons etc between the larger stations. In 1966 BR's own parcels business was separated from the general-merchandise sundries traffic, allowing it to concentrate on the brand of Red Star parcels, still essentially a station-to-station service; heavier or bulkier items went to the remaining Sundries Division, which became National Freight Carriers. *The Revd Alan Newman*

Right: Having penetrated deep into Southern territory with the previous day's Severn Tunnel Junction–Poole working, No D815 *Druid* is now returning through the New Forest near Brokenhurst with the corresponding service back to Severn Tunnel in May 1967. This out-and-back service served the yards at Bournemouth, Eastleigh and Poole, while a separate overnight service from the WR, also booked for a 'Warship', ran to Weymouth via the GW route, the locomotive returning on an early-morning Weymouth–Bristol passenger working. *Derek Cross*

Left: No D6314 hugs the Tamar estuary with a trip working returning to Tavistock Junction yard from the munitions store at Ernesettle on 31 July 1968. This train, which was usually in the hands of an NBL Type 2 (Class 22), brought in fresh supplies and returned 'lifed' equipment from Naval vessels that were moored at the end of the long jetty. Travelling south on the old LSWR route, it is about to pass under the Royal Albert Bridge before swinging up to join the GWR route at St Budeaux. *Alistair Jeffery*

Above: No D6344 heads away from Shillamill Tunnel (visible in the distance) and makes for Tavistock North on the old LSWR route with a Plymouth–Exeter service on 18 April 1963. After the savage winter, the countryside still exhibits a bare look, the trees being devoid of any foliage to confirm the arrival of spring. This section of line, which was closed in 1968, is currently the subject of plans to re-lay the track between Bere Alston and Tavistock; this may return Tavistock, which once boasted two stations, to the national network, allowing commuting into Plymouth by rail once again. *John Beckett*

31

Above left: Standing in the yard at Swindon Works on 17 June 1962 is No D602 *Bulldog*. The locomotive now has revised grilles supplying air to the cooler groups, while a yellow panel, with top edges sloping to a gentle peak, has been applied. However, four-digit roller blinds, by this date a standard fitment on new locomotives, have yet to be added. *Mike Pope*

Left: No D602 had gained Rail blue by the time it was allocated to Landore for a brief spell working in Wales along with Nos D601/4, which remained green until withdrawal. In September 1967, far from its usual haunts, *Bulldog* runs round its train at Llandrindod Wells, on the Central Wales line, before returning south with the 'as required' trip freight to Llandeilo Junction. It was hoped that their relatively heavy

weight would make the A1A-A1A 'Warships' useful substitutes for English Electric Type 3 diesel-electrics (Class 37s), but they would return to Laira after barely three months. *Roy Palmer*

Above: Last of the A1A-A1A 'Warships', No D604 *Cossack*, arrives at Redruth on 19 August 1967 with train 1V33, the southbound 'Cornishman'. This was one of the very few passenger turns still booked for a '600' between Plymouth and Penzance, which perhaps explains why so few photographs were taken of these locomotives in their later years; almost all their other duties involved freight or parcels. Only four months from withdrawal, No D604 looks in very good condition in green livery, having received its last repaint at Swindon in September 1966. *Peter Gray*

Left: A delightful scene conveying the feel of the deserted moorland landscape near Yarde, in North Devon, as No D6320 approaches from the Torrington direction with a short train to collect further ball clay from the workings at Marland (near Petrockstow) and Meeth on 23 March 1967. The embankment on which the train is travelling hides a trestle viaduct of the narrow-gauge line that had been built by the Marland Light Railway for transporting china clay. In the years 1922-5 the line was converted to standard gauge and extended southwards from Torrington to Halwill Junction. It was by now known as the North Devon & Cornwall Junction Light Railway (ND&CJLR) — a little confusing, as the full 21-mile route from Torrington to Halwill Junction was within the county of Devon; the reference to Cornwall was that at Halwill Junction the ND&CJLR connected with the existing LSWR lines to Bude and Padstow, each of which quickly led into Cornwall. *Alistair Jeffery*

Above: On New Year's Day 1968 No D862 *Viking* leaves St Blazey behind as it sets off with sheeted clay on the direct route to the docks at Fowey. The train is travelling on the line, dedicated to clay traffic, that was to close later that year, being converted into a private roadway for the sole use of English China Clays (ECC). Once closure had been effected the rail traffic was diverted to the old passenger line which ran down the estuary via Golant from Lostwithiel. Operationally this was a much longer route and to this day requires trains from the principal clay-producing area to use the main line in a steep climb to Treverrin Tunnel before dropping down to Lostwithiel, where the locomotive must run round to gain access to the Fowey branch. The wooden-bodied wagons seen here date from the late 1950s and were maintained by the wagon works at St Blazey. At this date the clay was simply sheeted over; not until the early 1970s were the tarpaulins usually pitched as a tent, to try to prevent ingress of water and other contaminants. *Alistair Jeffery*

This scene, recorded from the footbridge leading to Laira, confirms the depot's status as the principal hydraulic facility in the West of England. All of the main-line types are visible on 1 October 1967. Closest is No D6314, the first of four NBL Type 2s painted in blue with small warning panels. Beyond stands No D603 *Conquest* in green, while to the right is No D600 *Active*, in blue and sporting full yellow ends. Other locomotives outside the light-servicing shed include 'Westerns', 'Warships', further NBL Type 2s and a single 'Hymek'. Laira was the prototype for large WR diesel depots and was purpose-built on a fresh site near the old steam shed. The heavy-maintenance hall was a particularly impressive concrete building with barrel-vault roofing and split-level facilities. The depot, which maintained locomotives and DMUs, was opened fully in late 1961. *Russell Leitch*

The diesel depot at St Blazey was converted from the old steam shed, the half roundhouse being used to berth locomotives under cover. It provided light servicing for locomotives involved in the extensive china-clay operations as well as passenger services to Newquay during the summer. Tucked away in the roundhouse on 20 September 1967 are three of the Pilot Scheme North British Type 2s, Nos D6303/1/2, all in different liveries. The locomotives were formally allocated to Laira, where major maintenance work was undertaken, but were nominally based at St Blazey. Being significantly different from the production series of NBL Type 2s, Nos D6300-5 were early victims of 'rationalisation', No D6301 becoming the first casualty, at the end of 1967, the other five all being condemned in May 1968. *Russell Leitch*

Left: When Swindon started painting 'Hymeks' in blue, at the end of 1966, the first (No D7033) was given full yellow ends in a style only subtly different from that finally adopted. The next three to be repainted (Nos D7004, D7007 and D7051) emerged with small yellow panels, the blue extending around the window area. Thus adorned, No D7007 is seen on 26 October 1971 approaching the Dundas Aqueduct in the Limpley Stoke valley with the 09.15 Cardiff–Portsmouth. In those days paint was not as durable as it is today, and after four years the red-oxide undercoat has worn through in a number of areas. *Ivo Peters*

Above: After just three repaints it was decided that plain blue looked rather drab compared with the original green livery, on which the window surrounds had been picked out in a pale grey (looking almost white). In an attempt to improve the appearance Swindon's painters reverted to finishing the window-frame area in 'off white' on the next 14 repaints in blue. Although not part of the corporate livery this was an embellishment that would find favour several years later on Finsbury Park's 'Deltics' and a handful of Class 33s. No D7046 shows off its 'white' window frames as it climbs away from Bath with the 09.50 Cardiff–Portsmouth on 10 June 1968. *The Revd Alan Newman*

Resting 'on the blocks' at Paddington, No D1039 *Western King* has arrived in the capital with the 06.45 from Newton Abbot on 16 April 1970. The locomotive gained full yellow ends while still in maroon during a visit to Swindon in April 1968. It remained in this livery until November 1970, when a further call to works saw it emerge three months later in standard blue. *Hugh Dady*

Nowadays part of the National Collection, No D1023 *Western Fusilier* gets into its stride passing through Sydney Gardens, Bath, with the 09.40 Weston-super-Mare–Paddington on 3 May 1968. Although it was not originally intended to allow the 'iron road' through the gardens, which had been planted in the early 18th century, the railway was eventually made a feature for the public to observe, with elegant bridges and short tunnels under the roadways at either end. *The Revd Alan Newman*

Left: 'Hymeks' were not as common on the Berks & Hants as were the larger Type 4s, but they did put in appearances on engineers' trains and the Summer Saturday service from Paddington to Ilfracombe. On Wednesday 6 August 1969 one of the early blue repaints makes its way west past the pumping station at Crofton with a short ballast train, probably returning from Reading Yard. *Alistair Jeffery*

Above: Passengers await developments at Ilfracombe on 27 July 1968 as No D7036 pushes back the stock of the 08.05 from Paddington prior to running round its train. The few locomotive-hauled services still surviving by this date were mainly in the hands of 'Warships', although this Saturdays-only service and the 15.05 return working to Paddington would often produce a 'Hymek'. The exceptionally steep climb of 1 in 36 out of the station and the twisting nature of the line up to Mortehoe meant that the nine-coach load would present quite a challenge for the 1,700hp locomotive. *Alistair Jeffery*

The doyen of the 'Hymek' class takes the chord at Bradford Junction with an additional northbound coal working on 20 October 1969. No D7000 had been delivered in April 1961 in BR Brunswick green with a lime-green band along the bottom edge of the bodysides (as on the 'Deltics') and off-white window surrounds. Yellow panels were applied subsequently, and in September 1968 the locomotive received full yellow ends, remaining in this condition until outshopped in August 1970 in standard blue (with full yellow ends). Based latterly at Old Oak Common, it would be withdrawn on 30 July 1973. *The Revd Alan Newman*

Bound for the power station at Portishead, No D1040 *Western Queen* approaches Freshford with a lengthy coal train from Radstock on the afternoon of 27 January 1969. At the time this was a daily flow from the North Somerset coalfield and was usually powered by a 'Warship' or 'Western', but it was destined to cease altogether upon closure of the coalfield in 1973. When the picture was taken No D1040 had just been reallocated to Bristol Bath Road, joining 11 sisters, but its stay was brief, and it returned to Laira in May 1969. However, Bath Road would remain home to a stud of around a dozen Class 52s until October 1971, following which the entire fleet was concentrated at Laira. *The Revd Alan Newman*

Above: As was the case with other classes, initial repaints of 'Westerns' in blue featured small yellow warning panels rather than full yellow ends, seven examples being so treated. Here No D1037 *Western Empress* hurries the down 'Cornish Riviera' past the junction for Frome at Clink Road on 25 September 1970. Also photographing the scene, but in black & white, is Ivo Peters, visible on the embankment (right). The locomotive's blue livery had been applied during an 'Intermediate' repair at Swindon in January 1967 and would last until a repaint with full yellow ends in June 1971. *The Revd Alan Newman*

Right: No D1065 *Western Consort* arrives at Castle Cary, junction for the GW route to Weymouth, with the 07.53 Paignton–Paddington on 18 September 1974. This was one of two services, the other being the 05.05SX Plymouth–Paddington, that were booked to call at the Somerset station from the start of the 1974 summer timetable; together with return trains leaving Paddington at 16.30 and 18.30 these gave Castle Cary its first direct service to/from the capital. At this time the coal yard was still active, access being controlled by the backing signal (with holes in its arm), while above the first coach is the functional but unattractive flat-roofed signalbox, constructed during the war years after enemy action in 1942 destroyed much of the junction and original GW signalbox. The station remains important for South Somerset today, being the closest rail link to Glastonbury, Street and Wells. *John Vines*

Left: In the late 1960s No D6333 was one of a number of NBL Type 2s based at Newton Abbot and was often employed on the milk trains from Exeter to Chard, Hemyock and Torrington. Here it is seen shunting in the sidings for the Unigate dairy at Hemyock on 19 April 1969. The branch known as the Culm Valley line began at Tiverton Junction, and although the last passenger train ran on 7 September 1963 the line would survive on a freight-only basis for a further 12 years. Initially the preserve of a 'D2xxx' diesel-mechanical shunter, it was strengthened to take a 'D63xx' from the mid-1960s. In the absence of station staff the crew were expected to open and close all the level crossing gates as they proceeded up the valley, with the result that delivering the empties and collecting the loaded tanks remained an all-day job from Exeter. The line's fate was sealed by closure of the dairy in 1975. *Bernard Mills*

Above: Blue-liveried No D6336 eases gently away from the Royal Albert Bridge, having crossed into Devon with a lengthy freight from Liskeard bound for Tavistock Yard on 31 July 1968. This was a daily working, as were other mixed freights from Truro and Ponsandane, but over the next 15 years all of this traffic, along with the perishables and milk would be lost to road hauliers. In common with those locomotives delivered with split headcode boxes (Nos D6334-57), No D6336 has retained its plain two-piece gangway doors. Surprisingly, given their limited use, the doors on many earlier examples were rebuilt to fold in on themselves, giving the appearance of four vertical segments, and differing positions of headcode boxes, lights and grabrails ensured much variety within the class. *Alistair Jeffery*

Above: No D846 *Steadfast* climbs through the wooded avenue on Honeybourne Bank with the 16.15 Worcester–Paddington in early May 1970. Just a few days later, on 23 May, the locomotive caught fire near Stoke Cannon while working the 09.30 Paddington–Paignton. The ferocity of the blaze prevented it from being uncoupled from the train, and by the time the fire brigade had extinguished the flames No D846 had suffered severe damage. This required a trip to Swindon, where it would lose its early blue livery, with BR emblem above the nameplate. Following overhaul the locomotive was reallocated to Newton Abbot, where it remained until withdrawal on 22 May 1971. *Gerry Batchelor*

Right: No D835 *Pegasus* approaches Chalbury with the 14.15 Worcester–Paddington in June 1970. At this date the Paddington–Worcester service was shared by Class 43s (usually from Old Oak Common or Newton Abbot), Class 35s and 47s. Despite a subsequent visit to Swindon, where it received a fresh coat of blue, No D835 would last barely another year, being withdrawn in the major hydraulic cull of 3 October 1971. *Gerry Batchelor*

The Beeching vision for the freight business was for it to concentrate on block and company trains using modern air-braked stock. This put the vacuum-braked diesel-hydraulics at something of a disadvantage, which was magnified by the move towards air-braking for passenger stock. The cramped internal layout of the hydraulic classes left little room for the addition of air-braking equipment, and in the event only the 'Westerns' would be so equipped. The old order is represented by this view of No D1054 *Western Governor* negotiating Bradford Junction with a partially vacuum-fitted train on 6 June 1969. The locomotive would visit Swindon in September 1970 for dual braking as part of the DAB/AWS modification programme.
The Revd Alan Newman

Approaching Bathampton Junction, where the line to Westbury branches off, No D1020 *Western Hero* heads a smart rake of Mk 1 stock making up a mid-morning Bristol–Paddington service on 13 June 1969. Competition with the M4 motorway was now intense, and each year British Rail tried to shave a minute or two from the schedule. At this date the train was vacuum-braked, but the introduction of air-braked stock would see a number of diagrams turned over to Class 47s by the following year. No D1020 was one of four 'Westerns' that remained vacuum-only as time and money ran out for the dual-brake conversion programme. Along with Nos D1017-9 it thus became a candidate for early withdrawal, succumbing in June 1973.
The Revd Alan Newman

A sharp shower has done little to remove the build-up of grime on No D1045 *Western Viscount*, pictured just after servicing in the through-road shed at Old Oak Common on 25 April 1970. Its condition is typical of a period during which the external cleaning of locomotives was seemingly accorded a low priority by the 'owning' depot. No D1045 had since June 1965 been based at Laira, where it would remain allocated until withdrawal in December 1974. *Hugh Dady*

Resplendent in the final version of blue applied to the Class 22s, with numbers under the BR emblem, No 6326 stands on one of the turntable roads at Old Oak Common depot on Saturday 25 April 1970. Only the previous Wednesday the locomotive was noted undergoing tests outside the weigh shop at Swindon, so its condition here is pretty close to 'ex works'. Only eight locomotives were treated to this version of blue livery; indeed, just over half the class were withdrawn while still in green. No 6326 had a long association with the London Division, being in 1964 the first of its type to be transferred from the West of England for empty-carriage-stock duties at Paddington. *Hugh Dady*

Above: In the weak light of early morning No D1003 *Western Pioneer* waits to run round the 00.50 Paddington–Milford Haven sleeping-car train at Carmarthen on 3 August 1974. Although this was quite often 'Western'-hauled from Paddington as far as Swansea the final stretch was usually in the hands of a Class 37, but No D1003 had been provided by Landore for the remainder of the journey via Whitland and Clarbeston Road. *Tony Wardle*

Left: Although most commonly associated with the line to Fishguard Harbour, hydraulics appeared on all three lines in West Wales and on summer Saturdays could be found on the branch to Pembroke Dock, which diverged from the Fishguard route at Whitland. This view at Tenby features No D1022 *Western Sentinel* in charge of a Paddington–Pembroke Dock service, probably during the summer of 1973. *Andrew Vines collection*

One route with which 'Hymeks' were associated throughout their lives was the cross-country Cardiff–Portsmouth Harbour corridor via Bristol, Salisbury and Southampton, on which the first examples, delivered new to Bristol Bath Road, were quickly put to work. Save for a brief spell in 1966, when WR 'Inter-City' DMUs were tried, there remained a small core of locomotive-hauled through services to the South Coast which would remain the preserve of 'Hymeks' until 1973, when declining numbers saw the hydraulics hand over to Class 31s and 47s. From the mid-1960s, as service frequency gradually increased, the length of trains was reduced from nine or 10 coaches to five- or six-coach formations. On 10 April 1970 No D7096 speeds through Avoncliff with the 09.35 Cardiff–Portsmouth. *The Revd Alan Newman*

57

Above: On 25 September 1970 No D7041 heads east from the Frome line at Clink Road Junction with a lengthy freight, the consist including a number of wagons released from repair at the Radstock wagon works. Established in the days of the GWR and S&DR, the works carried out repairs, particularly to the brakes, running gear and rigging, on a diverse array of types ranging from ballast wagons, including Walrus, Dogfish and Grampus, to BR 16-ton mineral wagons and a variety of tank wagons, several examples of which may be seen here. No D7041 was one of the last members of the initial batch of 'Hymeks' (Nos D7000-44), ordered in June 1959 at a price of £80,000 each. *The Revd Alan Newman*

Right: On 6 July 1971 No D7015 climbs through a cutting south of Wanstrow, on the branch from Witham Friary, with bitumen tanks *en route* from Avonmouth to Cranmore. Bitumen is the heaviest fraction produced by the refining of crude oil, and each tank wagon has a gas- or oil-fed burner used to thin the oil in the discharge operation. Most of the bitumen delivered to the depot at Cranmore was mixed with aggregate to produce asphalt for surfacing Somerset's road network. A Bristol Bath Road locomotive when photographed, No D7015 would be withdrawn in less than a year, succumbing in June 1972. *Ivo Peters*

In the soft evening light of 1 July 1969 No D829 *Magpie* pulls away from Westbury with the 17.00 Paignton–Paddington. Within a few weeks the locomotive would be admitted to Swindon for overhaul, emerging in a fresh coat of blue. *Magpie* had two principal claims to fame. In May 1961 it attended the Institute of Locomotive Engineers' Golden Jubilee celebrations at Marylebone, following which HRH The Duke of Edinburgh, who had opened the event, was given a cab ride and apparently allowed to take part in driving the locomotive to Windsor. In later years it was adopted by the ITV children's programme *Magpie*, BBC rival *Blue Peter* having done likewise with the 'A2' Pacific of that name. *The Revd Alan Newman*

They don't come any cleaner than this! In what can only be described as mint condition following a spell in Swindon Works, No 839 *Relentless* slogs up the final 1-in-37 climb to the summit at Dainton with an empty-stock working from Newton Abbot to Laira on Sunday 12 July 1970. Collected from Swindon earlier that day, it had until recently been one of a final handful of Class 43s still running in maroon with yellow panels, but in the early summer of 1970, along with several other North British 'Warships' that were expected to be withdrawn, it was instead authorised for overhaul to help alleviate the WR's motive-power shortage.
J. M. Boyes / Armstrong Railway Photographic Trust

With only a few days left in traffic, No 867 *Zenith* finds employment taking a breakdown crane from Bristol to Didcot, and approaches Shrivenham on 7 October 1971. Having been the last of the Swindon-built 'Warships' to retain maroon with yellow panels, *Zenith* was repainted in blue during a very brief visit to Swindon in early September 1970. It thus ran for barely a year in this livery, being withdrawn officially on 18 October 1971 after a career of just 10½ years. *The Revd Alan Newman*

No D6340 of Old Oak Common finds itself on an unusual duty, heading along the down fast at Moreton Cutting, east of Didcot, with a rake of 10 Mk1 coaches on Saturday 15 June 1968. The headcode displayed provides little clue as to the working, which was possibly the result of a failure or displaced stock due to recent ASLEF action. At this time the Class 22s were regulars on empty-stock duties between Paddington and Old Oak Common, but their appearance with such a load on the main line was exceptional. *Bryan Hicks*

Brunel's Clifton Suspension Bridge over the Avon Gorge provides an elegant backdrop to one of Bristol Bath Road's 'Hymeks' pottering along the branch from Portishead on 20 February 1970. The short train of chemical tanks was carrying phosphoric acid from the Albright & Wilson chemical plant. The branch from Parsons Street finally closed to freight traffic in April 1981 and was mothballed, but following extensive track renewal it was reopened early in 2002 to serve the growing Portbury Dock and now conveys mainly coal and imported cars.
The Revd Alan Newman

With a large glass area but no external doors, the well-sealed 'Western' cab could become very hot in summer, and in 1971 five Class 52s (Nos D1012/28/39/56/71) were fitted with a square vent on the cab front, in an attempt to improve ventilation. However, this was considered to offer no real improvement, and the modification was not extended to the rest of the class. On 28 August 1975 No D1071 *Western Renown* rests at St Blazey depot, the vent being clearly visible. *Trevor Maxted*

No D1058 *Western Nobleman* leads No 816 *Eclipse* on the descent into Totnes with train 6B64, the St Blazey–Avonmouth mixed goods, on 13 September 1971. Semaphore signals are still in place, but the telegraph poles present in 1969 (and featured on page 54 of *The Heyday of the Warships*) have been swept away, the cables being now concealed underground in trunking. The train was usually 'Warship'-hauled, and the addition of No D1058 was probably a convenient way of moving the 'Western' up to Exeter or Bristol. *David Pool*

Left: Although the 'Westerns' are generally associated with the stone trains from the Mendip quarries these workings were shared in the early days with 'Warships', particularly when SR crews already had traction knowledge on the Class 42s. A flow that was quite regularly 'Warship'-hauled was that from Westbury to Gatwick or Merstham for construction of the M23 and M25 motorways. On a fine July day in 1972 No 812 *Royal Naval Reserve 1859-1959* rounds the curve from Shalford Junction, south of Guilford, and begins to traverse the North Downs line to Redhill with train 6O14, the 08.55 Westbury–Gatwick. Foster Yeoman originally had its own fleet of wooden-bodied wagons but disposed of these after World War 2 when it switched largely to road haulage; when it reverted to rail in 1969 BR supplied a

number of second-hand types including, as seen here, reconditioned HTV wagons, more commonly associated with the movement of coal. Even with roller bearings and vacuum braking the payload was limited to 25 tons, with the result that the hoppers often appeared only half full. *Trevor Maxted*

Above: On 18 September 1971 No D7026 pulls away from Christchurch, on the Southern Region's South Western Division, with the 09.30 Birmingham New Street–Poole, passing '3-TC' trailer unit No 301 at the rear of a Weymouth–Waterloo working. No D7026 would survive until October 1974 and at one stage was seriously considered as a preservation candidate. *David Pool*

Left: The 'Westerns' began their lives with ambitious two/three-day cyclic diagrams starting from their base at Laira. These included a run up to the capital followed by duties on the old Great Western route from London to the Midlands via Saunderton. The summer of 1962 saw two diesel-hauled services on the Paddington–Wolverhampton line, the class taking over fully in September 1962, but such exploits were to be short-lived; in 1964 the route north of Banbury came under London Midland Region control, the 'Westerns' being swifly displaced by Brush Type 4s, and only towards the end of their lives, from the 1973 summer timetable, did they reappear regularly on the Paddington–Birmingham corridor. On 4 September 1975 No D1071 *Western Renown* approaches Small Heath station with the 18.25 Birmingham–Paddington. The locomotive and stock had earlier worked up to the Midland city with the 14.05 from Paddington, this being one of four out-and-back diagrams to which Class 52s were often allocated at this time. *Michael Mensing*

Above: A typical scene from the mid-1970s features one of the Laira 'Westerns' passing Woodborough with the 10.30 Newquay–Paddington on 9 August 1975. At this time the semaphore signalling for the loops was still intact, and a yellow BR van can be seen sharing parking space with what was probably the signalman's Morris Marina car. The presence of concrete troughing signifies that the days of telegraph poles will shortly come to an end. *John Spencer Gilks*

69

Rarely recorded on film was the replenishment of water tanks on first-generation diesels from the water columns installed for steam locomotives. On 28 March 1963 the driver of No D838 *Rapid* takes advantage of this facility at Bristol Temple Meads before the locomotive departs westward with the 05.30 Paddington–Plymouth.

The B-B 'Warships' had a water capacity of 940 gallons which supplied the train-heating boiler — in the case of this and other NBL-built examples a Spanner Mk 1a. *Russell Leitch*

Steam billows from the boiler of No D1057 *Western Chieftain* as the locomotive awaits a delayed departure from Bristol Temple Meads with the 08.35 Paddington–Plymouth on Sunday 26 October 1975. Equipping the 'Westerns' to supply electric train heating proved impossible, there being insufficient room for a separately driven generator in addition to the boiler. The already cramped internal layout had been further cluttered by the equipment needed for the dual-braking programme, which had seen the capacity of both water and fuel tanks reduced in an effort to provide space. *David Pool*

No D7066 arrives at Southampton on 22 September 1971 with the 09.30 Birmingham New Street– Poole — one of several inter-regional workings that involved a change of locomotive at Reading. No D7066 was very near the end of its career, being one of the early withdrawals at the end of November; the 'Hymek' run-down began in September, and by the end of the year 17 of the class had been culled. The pace of withdrawal continued in 1972, during which a further 62 were removed from traffic, but slowed thereafter, and more than two years would elapse before all of the remaining 22 had been whittled away. *David Pool*

Many readers will have spent at least a few hours viewing trains from the platforms of Berkshire's transport capital, and some will doubtless remember the lady announcer's voice of the early 1970s echoing from the tannoys: "Reading, this is Reading; fast train to London — Platform 5". Besides an endless procession of InterCity services the interested observer could watch a variety of freight traffic, which was usually routed through the slow lines or sometimes around the back of the station. On the morning of 23 May 1972, just six weeks before withdrawal, No D7038 approaches from the west with a lengthy mixed freight from South Wales bound for the Eastern Region, probably Temple Mills. *Paul Townsend*

Left: On summer Saturdays some locomotive-hauled trains from London to Paignton continued on to Kingswear, until closure of the line south of Goodrington in 1972. At this time also certain Saturday services to the West Country started from Ealing or Slough, as the stock could run straight from Old Oak Common and thus alleviate congestion at Paddington. Reaching journey's end on 21 June 1969, No D1043 *Western Duke* enters Kingswear with the 08.42 from Ealing, the estuary of the River Dart (seen left) being the third major estuary encountered since the train left Exeter. The locomotive had begun its spell in blue in late 1966 with small yellow panels but following collision repairs was outshopped from Swindon in December 1968 with standard full yellow ends. *Gerry Batchelor*

Above: Sun, sea, sand and a railway line worked by 'Westerns' were ingredients that appealed to many enthusiasts in the mid-1970s. While the 'Warships' and North British Type 2s had slipped away almost unnoticed, a sleeping interest had been awakened as the 'Westerns' entered their final years. By 1973 locomotive overhauls at Swindon had ceased, and it was left to Laira to keep the fleet running as best it could, initially with a limited supply of overhauled components from the works and latterly by cannibalisation of early withdrawals. To keep the class looking presentable the depot embarked upon a repainting programme, which saw more than 50 examples spruced up in the period 1973-6. On 27 August 1975 No D1009 *Western Invader*, still fresh from a repaint, approaches Rockstone Bridge, Dawlish, with the 13.30 Paddington–Penzance. *Hugh Dady*

Pictured near Albury in September 1972, No 810 *Cockade* has the stiffest part of the climb from Chilworth behind it as it heads the 08.55 Westbury–Gatwick stone train towards Gomshall, on the North Downs line. This duty was most likely to produce a Class 42 or 47, although in later years a few Class 52s worked over the route, usually with trains for Ardingly. In the early 1970s the line also had a regular 'Hymek' diagram, this being a Bradford–Redhill parcels train which the hydraulics worked forward from Reading.
Trevor Maxted

Towards the end of its BR career No 7017 was subjected to a depot repaint during which the opportunity was taken to remove the cast numerals and replace them, under the driver's window only, with standard white adhesive digits. On 21 August 1974, during its final summer in BR service, No 7017 rounds the Greenford loop at West Ealing with a lengthy freight from Park Royal to Acton Yard. The locomotive subsequently became the first 'Hymek' to enter preservation, being transferred in March 1976 to its new home at Minehead, on the West Somerset Railway.
Hugh Dady

On 4 September 1976 No D1048 *Western Lady* has charge of the 10.55 Acton–Norwood, seen approaching Latchmere Junction signalbox, which was being repainted at the time. Technically still on LMR metals, the train will shortly pass under the complex of lines to the north of Clapham Junction and join the Central Division of the Southern Region. Such locomotive diagramming was practical only if the crew's roster would allow an out-and-back working from the Western Region. *Hugh Dady*

As the 'Westerns' began their final summer the demand for special workings increased, although few observers were prepared for the last frenetic round of specials at the end of the year. No D1013 *Western Ranger* became an instant celebrity when, in May 1976, it emerged from Laira with a red background to its name- and numberplates. For locomotives outshopped in Rail blue Swindon used black for name- and numberplates, adhering to the specification laid down by the design consultants responsible for BR's corporate image. Others, however, had different ideas, among them Laira's then depot engineer, recently transferred from the

Eastern Region, where it had become the norm for nameplates to be backed in flame red; if this colour was acceptable for a 'Deltic' or a 'Peak' then why not for a 'Western'? The embellishment on No D1013, which the locomotive retained until withdrawal, remained unique within the 'Western' fleet, although 'Warship' No 818 *Glory* had earlier received similar treatment for its final three months in service. Negotiating Aller Junction on a fine evening in June 1976, *Western Ranger* heads for Exeter with a local working from Paignton. *Mike Pope*

After the rather lukewarm response by enthusiasts to the withdrawal of 'Warships' and 'Hymeks' British Rail understandably underestimated the demand for farewell tours behind the 'Westerns', and it fell largely left to private individuals to fill the gap. The autumn of 1976 simply did not provide enough weekends to satisfy demand for charter trains, and, after a break over the Christmas period, specials continued through January 1977 and into the last month of hydraulics on BR. The original RPPR 'Western Requiem', taking a 'Western' for a last run up some of the Welsh valley lines, was sold out within days, and organiser John Vaughan was quick to arrange a relief train, which in the event ran a week earlier than that originally scheduled! On 13 February 1977 the 'relief', headed by No D1010 *Western Campaigner*, passes permanent-way staff as the driver applies the power through Quakers Yard *en route* to Treherbert, Merthyr and Aberdare. Leaning from the forward engine-room window is the travelling fitter, while heads seem to have bagged a spot at most of the carriage windows. *Mike Pope*

No D1015 *Western Champion* is well known today, beautifully restored to run on the national network by members of the Diesel Traction Group (DTG). However, towards the end of its BR career the locomotive did not seem a likely candidate for preservation, despite its interesting history of wearing the experimental golden-ochre livery. Here a weary-looking No D1015 waits to head west from Paddington on Sunday 3 October 1976. Standing in the distance is No D1001 *Western Pathfinder* with train 1B79, the 23.15 Paddington–Penzance newspapers. Sadly this locomotive would not complete its journey that night; south of Stoke Cannon, on the approach to Exeter, it struck an engineers' van which had stalled on a farm crossing, and the damage sustained by the locomotive led inevitably to its withdrawal. No D1015 was, of course, more fortunate and is today the only example of a main-line-registered hydraulic for current generations to ride behind and enjoy. *Mike Pope*